A
Legal
Primer
for
Independent
Schools

Albrecht Saalfield

Center for Teaching
The Westminster Schools

National Association of Independent Schools
18 Tremont Street, Boston, Massachusetts 02108

P
379.3
Saalfield

purt. 7.75
1/13/86

Contents

Acknowledgment

I thank the following people for their thoughtful and generous assistance generally and in the specific areas of their expertise: Colin Irving, business manager, Phillips Exeter Academy (N.H.); Barbara F. Luehning, principal, Seaford (Del.) High School, who provided most of the glossary; Rowland P. McKinley, Jr., headmaster, University High School (Ohio); and John Mason, of the law firm of Ropes and Gray, in Boston. Without the contributions, review, and encouragement of this "committee of readers," this text would have been far more difficult to produce.

Preface

Ours seems to be an increasingly litigious society — and independent schools are increasingly involved in litigation. NAIS has entered into this arena quite hesitantly, even though the need for some guidelines has been evident for a long time. It is important for users and readers of this manual to understand that hesitancy.

For one thing, NAIS does not and must not practice law; not only is it inappropriate, it is misleading, for differing situations and cases require that each school use its own legal counsel. For another, the law is a living, changing set of rules that enable society to govern itself. Even as the ink dries on this page, some of the laws cited here may be superseded and others newly interpreted by the courts.

Thus in publishing this book NAIS is in no way entering the practice of law, nor does it assume any responsibility for the consequences of a school's following guidelines given here. The word "primer" has been carefully chosen to denote a book of elementary principles, offered to provide general background reading, to alert independent school people to things they should know, to suggest, and to help prevent. Although some of the author's examples may seem extreme, we think the consequences of ignorance of the law can be so great that they are included.

We are impressed by the book's illumination of the ideals or standards by which a good independent school is operated. The law emerges not as an incursive or encroaching force but as a guarantor of minimum and sensible standards beyond which most schools operate anyway, as the author suggests. This accords with basic NAIS philosophy with respect to the law and to government: to view requirements not with anger or fear but with awareness; to deal from a position of political, personal, and informational relationship to civil authority; and to conduct our affairs so impeccably that we are absolutely above reproach with respect to the law and society's expectations.

We think the primer contributes to that purpose; we think it is conducive to even better schools.

John C. Esty, Jr.
President, NAIS

Introduction

The purpose of this "primer" is to provide general familiarity with laws and their effect, or potential effect, on independent schools and on the people involved with them. Such familiarity should help readers spot legal problems and prepare for or, better, prevent them. Because federal and state laws change, laws vary from state to state, and facts vary from case to case, generalizations are made here simply to signal areas of concern, not as definitive statements.

NAIS sees this book as a desk reference on legal issues that will help to equip staff members, administrators, and trustees to understand better and face squarely what it means to be involved with an independent school at any level.

Although schools generally have higher ideals and objectives than those reflected in the minimum standards of laws, their procedures for attaining those objectives can sometimes cause legal difficulties. For this reason, the primer necessarily addresses policy issues as well as laws. Readers should remain aware of this distinction.

For example, any impulse to call a lawyer about school activities should be heeded, for a procedure that has potential for being weak legally probably also does not accord with the mission of the school. Similarly, the desire for legal counsel about day-to-day dealings between students and teachers might also be a warning that standards are not being carefully upheld or are being violated.

But accidents do occur, and even the best-intentioned people can make mistakes. Schools should have their own paid legal counsel from whom they seek advice as needed. We hope this book will help readers better understand certain details of the law and issues that may warrant advice of legal counsel. Although readers may be tempted to start by reading only those chapters that pertain directly to them, we recommend reading the entire book for a more complete view of the issues presented.

When do schools seek legal counsel? In 1980, 413 schools responded to NAIS survey questions about lawsuits and costs of counsel. Subjects of litigation, reported here in order of frequency, were: dismissed faculty members, 10; accident liability, 8; student dismissals, 7; age or sex discrimination, 6; breach of contract with suppliers and builders, 6; Department of Labor wage and hour disputes, 4; disputes over payment of town tax, 4; minority rights, involving one faculty and one student dismissal, 2; and "failure to educate," 2.

In the area of costs, 98 schools reported paying legal counsel up to $2,000 in 1980; 53 schools paid $2,000-$4,000; 51 schools paid $4,000-$6,000; and 28 schools paid over $6,000. It therefore seems clear that, in addition to having counsel available, schools should budget reasonable amounts for legal fees.

The Glossary of Legal Terms, which forms Appendix A, is intended to serve readers who are curious about such terms as "police power," "standard of care," and "due diligence and care." Appendix B contains an index to NAIS legislative memoranda, which have been prepared periodically since 1970 to describe and discuss many of the issues covered here.

Lawsuits are expensive and painful. We hope that this book will at least provide some preventive medicine.

1.

The Trustees

According to the NAIS *Trustee Handbook*, "The primary responsibility of the board of trustees of an independent school is to see to it that the institution operates in the best interests of its students, teachers, and parents. . . . The trustees are custodians of the integrity of the institution, of its standing and reputation built by the founders and those who have labored over the years. Trustees hold in trust the school's future as well as its present."

Charter

The official document under which a school and its trustees operate is the charter, which describes the institution, its purpose, its location, and the constituencies it serves. The charter also describes the school's incorporators and the manner of incorporation as well as the classes, or categories, of members of the corporation.

The charter, or articles of incorporation, must be filed in most states with the secretary of state and, in some states, with the local or state education agency. Although practice varies widely across the country, it is understood that states have the constitutional authority to require initial and later filings of charters because states, under their police powers, monitor independent schools at least in terms of the health and welfare of their students and, to a limited degree, for the quality of education they provide. Periodic filings may be bothersome, but they confer certain benefits, such as maintenance of tax-exempt status and, in some instances, free use of public school transportation by private school students.

By-laws

Supporting the charter in greater detail are the by-laws of the institution, which describe how governance of the legal entity is carried out. In a series of articles, the by-laws prescribe and specify, for example, who may be members of the corporation and how they may take actions; the composition and powers of the board of trustees and the committee and voting structures by which the board exercises its powers; and items addressing particular aspects of the institution, such as classes of trustees, personal conflict of interest on the part of trustees, disclosure requirements relating to trustees, and provisions for indemnification, or protection against damages in lawsuits.

Because the by-laws may be amended at any time to reflect the current needs and status of the institution, trustees should review them annually to make sure that they are up to date. The trustees should also review the school's charter from time to time to assure themselves that none of their activities or any of the by-laws is outside the published purpose of the school.

Allowing for the many variations among independent schools, it is nevertheless typical for a charter and by-laws to establish the board of trustees as the policy-making body that is responsible for overseeing, but not managing, the institution. The board and its committees thereby have the power and responsibility to see that the school's policies are carried out in all areas, whether admission and financial aid, fund management, buildings and grounds, or the curriculum.

The most important responsibility the board ever has is to hire and work with the head of the school. It is through this one person that the board's policies are articulated, and it is to this one person, as chief executive officer, that the board delegates enormous powers. The distinctions are large but the lines often thin between delegating and then ignoring or meddling. To ignore is unconscionable — and legally dangerous; to meddle is destructive. This issue should be addressed during the orientation of new board members.

Minutes

The third and most detailed set of documents related to the

governance of the institution are the minutes of meetings of the board of trustees and its committees. Beyond allowing for continuity of thought, discussion, and action, minutes also afford important protection to board members individually and as a group. For example, if an administrator or faculty member acts in a way that causes harm — loss or detriment — of any kind to another person and is clearly in violation of board policy, minutes of the meeting at which that policy was set forth could exonerate the board. We say "could," because this potential protection would melt if the person harmed could show that, though the board had promulgated the policy, it had failed in its duty to make sure that the policy was indeed carried out. In the rare case where the majority of board members vote to do something that later turns out to be wrong — contrary to state law, for example — those members listed in the minutes as voting against the act would be insulated from liability.

Other important examples of the value of minutes involve issues of conflict of interest, disclosure of interest, and abstention of a board member whenever the board is voting on something that would benefit the abstaining member personally — the lawyer whose firm is chosen to represent the school, the contractor whose firm is chosen to build the gym. When questions arise, minutes can provide the evidence that will settle them one way or the other.

Accountability

As those having the authority to set policy and the duty to oversee management of the institution, the trustees are accountable to a wide range of agencies and individuals, including but not limited to the state attorney general, donors, contractors, applicants, students and families (possibly both as a corporate body and as individual board members), one another, faculty members, and graduates of the school.

Clearly, the institution, which is the object of the board's trust, must not be allowed to run afoul of local, state, or federal laws, including tax codes, nor should it be allowed to violate its own publicized policies or procedures. By what legal standards are trustees measured?

A word about the United States Constitution is appropriate here. The Constitution is written to protect us as individuals from actions by the state; it does not protect us from one another. Further, the Constitution does not protect individuals from "bad acts" by a private institution. Where the Constitution does apply to institutions is a function of "state action," that is, whether the state's contribution and control so entangle it with the operations—plant, equipment, budget—of an allegedly private institution that a court could find the institution to be operating as if it were an agent of the state. For the state merely to charter an institution or monitor its activities does not count as state action (but see Chapter 4, on discipline and due process).

Aside from state involvement, numerous statutes do exist under which independent schools may be subject to government sanctions. For example, the federal Family Educational Rights and Privacy Act (the Buckley Amendment) does not apply to independent schools unless they or any of their students receive funds directly from the U.S. Department of Education.

At the same time, Title VII of the Civil Rights Act of 1964—the federal equal employment opportunity statute— prohibits all employers from discriminating in hiring, discharging, or otherwise adversely affecting the status of an employee on the basis of race, color, religion, sex, or national origin. Title VII, enforced by the federal Equal Employment Opportunity Commission, allows for money damages, not simply for canceling funds, against most private employers whether they receive government funds or not.

Along with standards set by federal and state constitutions and countless federal and state statutes, institutions are held accountable under the common law, a body of legal principles that has grown out of court holdings in settling disputes. Not surprisingly, the common law pertaining to property changes much more slowly than, for example, the common law that pertains to the law of torts, or civil wrongs. The findings of courts in a school's own state in the areas of property, contract, and tort law provide the principles that will most likely affect the school because these are the areas in which the school is most often involved. Tort law is changing especially rapidly because it casts an ever bigger net to include those even potentially liable and is dramatically increasing the amounts of money recoverable for damages.

In honoring the fiduciary relationship they have with their school—to carry out their duties in good faith—trustees must act out of honesty, loyalty, and due diligence and care on behalf of the object of their trust. What exactly is "due diligence and care"? It is based on what trustees know or should know about the school before trouble arises, no matter who they are or what else is going on in their own lives. The busy lawyer who misses meetings, the older member who claims ignorance of modern finance, and the student member whose interest is in altering parietal rules are all held to the same high standards of due diligence and care by a court.

Due diligence extends to mismanagement, or potential personal liability for personal negligence as a trustee. Due diligence also includes acts of omission, or nonmanagement, such as not supervising the institution's investment policy and thereby wasting significant growth opportunities, not carrying insurance, not paying employment taxes, or incurring penalties by failing to file with the appropriate tax agencies.

An area that encompasses the entire notion of fiduciary responsibility and its concomitant due diligence is conflict of interest and self-dealing, where one's own benefit prevails over duty to another. Generally speaking, conflict of interest comes into play when self-dealing is involved. For example, a school may have contractors, bankers, and lawyers on its board. It may also have these people's firms providing services to the school for pay. It is at meetings when this remuneration is considered that conflict of interest for the person involved can arise. At such meetings, at least the following should occur: the board should invoke the provision in the by-laws for disclosure of interest by board members, and the board members involved should temporarily absent themselves from the meeting and then abstain from voting. The minutes should reflect thorough discussion of how the board came to select a member's firm as a provider and stress the cost benefit to the school of choosing this particular provider over others in the area.

A concept akin to conflict of interest is the "corporate opportunity doctrine," which says that directors and trustees may not take personal advantage of inside information gathered as a result of board membership to acquire a personal advantage. An example of abuse of this doctrine would be for an individual board member to hear at a board meeting about a piece of property offered privately to the school and to arrange, for his or her own advantage, to have someone else buy the property before the school could tender an offer to the seller and then to sell it to the school at a profit.

After reading this litany of potential pitfalls and possible group and personal liabilities, trustees may be uneasy. They will be made even more uneasy by the addition of yet another responsibility: inquiring into the acts of past board members for which current members may in some cases become liable if they do not investigate and rectify a given situation as needed.

Interested and committed board members, especially those who benefit from thorough orientation, will know enough to ask questions about past and present dealings. They will attend meetings. If other demands become too great, they will regretfully but dutifully resign. During their tenure on the board, they will insist that board policies be clear, consistent, published, enforced, and in keeping with both the law and the school's charter.

It is well to remember—even though most trustees and schools that deserve their energies function at a much higher level than the law's minimum standards—that anyone can sue a school and its trustees. Even if the school wins, it is costly in time, money, and emotion. Boards should have paid counsel and use it when issues arise, without allowing lawyers to determine what kind of school they should have. Boards should also carry directors' and officers' insurance or a specially tailored trustee and personnel policy that provides protection under the school's indemnity coverage. It is important to note that such insurance includes the insurer's responsibility to pay legal fees for investigation and defense up to the limit of the policy.

2.

The Head
of the School

As the school's chief executive officer, the head manages information from day to day and from year to year in keeping with policy set by the trustees and under their supervision. The head communicates with many different people — trustees, faculty members, parents, students, applicants, graduates, townspeople — by gathering and giving information that all parties involved use for making plans and decisions.

From a legal point of view, clear, consistent, accurate information is vital to protect the school and its employees from liability. Accurate and honest information is an essential part of the head's duty to exercise prudence, due diligence, and care. Obviously, the head does not tell everyone everything; rather, he or she needs to make sure that the information on which any person relies is supportable. People who rely on incorrect or incomplete information to their detriment may have legal recourse against not only the school but its head, personally.

Hiring procedures and problems

In some schools, according to the terms of their charter, the board may have authority and responsibility for hiring at all levels. In most schools, however, the head is responsible for all hiring (and firing) of the school's "agents" — faculty and staff members.

Hiring offers a complex example of the head's responsibility for clear communication. Common sense tells us that hiring depends a great deal on gathering and communicating good information.

Various state and federal laws restrict an employer's inquiry into the background of potential employees. The rule of thumb for such inquiries is the "rational relationship" test: is the information sought rationally related to successful performance of the job the applicant seeks? Questions about sex, age, religion, and race fail this test and thus properly have no place on employment forms or in interviews and are protected against by the laws of most states, federal laws like the Equal Employment Opportunity Act of 1972, and by Title VII of the 1964 Civil Rights Act.

Some bona fide occupational qualifications (BFQ's) provide exceptions to these laws, however, in that they are rationally related to a specific task. Examples of BFQ's include the religious beliefs of applicants for faculty positions in some religiously affiliated schools, a specific physical handicap that would disqualify a coaching candidate, and establishing that applicants should be over eighteen and under seventy years of age.

As part of employment procedure, clear job descriptions are the head's first responsibility, followed by use of tools for decision making that hew closely to that purpose. In this connection, some general questions are acceptable, such as asking about criminal convictions, which generally reflect on the morality and reputation of the applicant. Other general questions are not acceptable, even though they may be important to the head who is looking for continuity in the faculty, such as asking a newly married female candidate whether she plans to have children.

In short, highly professional awareness of competence and the qualifications necessary for a given job to be done make the rational relationship test relatively easy to apply. In the case of specific questions unique to the school, the head should consult the school's attorney for an elaboration of federal laws and the laws of the state in which the school is located.

While asking an organization to compile information on race and age may seem antithetical to placing restrictions on making employment decisions, it is not; the actual purpose is to keep records, not to gather information for the school to use in deciding whether to hire a given candidate. Should the school err by asking questions that are not absolutely essential, that in itself would not necessarily be damaging if the school were sued. If the school consistently asked these questions and disappointed applicants could prove that, taken together, the questions led to a faculty whose composition clearly did not include women and minorities, for example, the possibility of successful litigation would be greatly increased.

To have standing, a disappointed teaching applicant must be a member of a "protected class" — protected by constitution or statute with regard to age, race, sex, and so on, must have applied for a job for which there was an opening, must have been rejected as an individual, must have been qualified for the job, and the school must have continued to advertise the position. If these standards are met in the case under consideration, then the burden of proof in the lawsuit shifts to the school to show that its decision not to employ the grievant was appropriately founded.

Somewhat ironically, a school head faces legal exposure for not asking appropriate questions and verifying the credentials of applicants. A complicated example of this situation might arise if a reasonably qualified candidate who was also a woman — a member of a protected class — complained that she did not get a job that was advertised because the school wanted a man. If close examination showed that the man's credentials had not been carefully reviewed, or were only loosely reviewed and were in fact less impressive than those of the disappointed woman, the school's defense in a sex discrimination suit would be severely weakened.

A head who fails to inquire whether an applicant has a criminal record might be liable for criminal acts committed by that person within the scope of his or her employment by the school, not only on the basis of "respondeat superior" — one's accountability as a superior — but also would be liable for failure to act with prudence and due diligence. An employer is not liable for the behavior of employees when they act outside the scope of their employment.

Employment contracts

Once a candidate has been interviewed and found acceptable, the head of the school typically explains the new employee's duties and benefits and offers a contract in the form of a short, relatively general letter of welcome. This contract, like any other, should contain a clear expression of the essence of the agreement, the duration, or end point, of the agreement (the school year, for example), and the consideration for the agreement (performance and pay).

Ideally, the contract should be accompanied by a document spelling out faculty responsibilities and the school's procedures for dealing with faculty members in formal terms. While such a handbook probably need not be painstakingly detailed, it must give reasonable guidance and notice to faculty members in their several roles and lay the foundation for fair and reasonable, as opposed to arbitrary and capricious, dealings between employer and employee. Simply to say, either in writing or verbally, that "all faculty members are expected to pull their weight" can lead to faculty claims of inequitable distribution of tasks and inequitable compensation. Such claims are not only disconcerting to all concerned but increasingly likely to reach a lawyer's office.

A school's employment contract should also spell out maternity, sabbatical, and sick leave policies, causes for termination or notice, and the procedures involved. Otherwise, these will be inferred from a school's practices over the years, and any inconsistencies, whether legitimate unto themselves or not, will put the school in a very weak position in litigation.

The contract with the head will of necessity be the broadest of all school employment contracts in its description of duties, but it should describe in detail duration and compensation, including perquisites, as well as termination procedures and the school's plan for compensating the head in the event of termination. The NAIS *Trustee Handbook* treats this matter at some length.

The head and the faculty

Tenure is one aspect of employment. Although few independent schools explicitly offer their employees tenure, the head of the school must be extremely careful not inadvertently to institute a system of "quasi tenure" by mentioning the elements of tenure in discussions of employment, even though not using the word "tenure" itself. Employees might well claim that they thought, from what the head said, that the school did have a tenure system and that they had made long-range plans accordingly, only to be terminated at the end of two or three years, "just when I was about to be paid what I'm really worth as a teacher."

Concerning termination more generally, if a school has sufficient confidence in its information about a teacher to terminate that teacher's contract, it should be willing to state the reasons to appropriate listeners — possible future employers of that same person, for example. Terms such as "lazy" and "not our type" are just as frustrating and uninformative in faculty evaluations as they are in student records. Worse, at least because they tend to ridicule the person described and almost certainly cost that person opportunities later on, they could be regarded as defamatory — libel if written, slander if spoken.

Truth is an almost perfect defense against charges of defamation. But even truth may cease to function as a shield if it is used widely and indiscriminately to make the person the object of ridicule. As a matter of law, an employer has a "qualified privilege" to discuss employees and, if malice is not involved, could mount a successful defense in a suit for defamation in most cases. As a matter of policy, the more precise an evaluation is, the more useful it is.

This raises the issue of the fiduciary responsibility that runs from the head to the faculty and staff of the school. As a matter of practical fact, in most schools the head is more powerful than any individual faculty member. Without exaggerating the head's role, it is clear that faculty members look to their chief executive for guidance, administrative skill, personal advice, and a degree of protection. A head who is trusted often is privy to considerable personal information about his or her colleagues. Inappropriate use of this information, especially if malice can be documented, could lead to charges of defamation or intentional infliction of emotional distress.

Schools are proud of their teachers individually and collectively, and they repeatedly say so. Applicants for admission, students, parents, donors, and others rely on these statements to be true, and they base certain decisions on them. If it can be shown, for example, not to be true that the school's tennis team is coached by four professionals, as stated, or that the science department really does not have three Ph.D.'s on its faculty, athletic hopefuls who have foregone opportunities at other schools or donors who have pledged gifts for the new science wing might have causes for legal action based on detrimental reliance and other "quasi contractual" theories that apply in instances where people act "as if" there were a contract.

Reliance can be based on any statement, not just one involving the quality of the faculty. The head of the school is responsible for making sure that all of the school's agents represent the school honestly. Thus the head should know what is being written and said by a desperate development officer, a zealous admission officer, an eager athletic director, or any other person who has the authority, or the apparent authority, to make representations about the school to the public.

In short, the head's role is all-encompassing. Instead of trying to cover everything related to the head in this chapter, various breaches of duty owed to those with whom the school comes in contact are dealt with in other chapters, depending on where such breaches are most likely to occur first.

3.

The Faculty

Faculty members should be aware that the courts also recognize that teachers have responsibilities as well as rights of their own. A faculty member's first responsibility is to the institution, then to the students as a group. Ethically and legally, it behooves each faculty member to know the limits of his or her authority — and personal skills and training — and to stay within those limits when dealing as a professional. For example, even though faculty contracts tend to be general, it is clear from them that a mathematics teacher is not also hired to be a psychiatrist or a coach also to be a reading specialist.

To state the issue somewhat differently, for all the positive and important roles teachers play, they are primarily agents of an institution. Starting with their employment contract and running through policies hammered out in curriculum, faculty, and staff committee meetings, faculty members must, individually and collectively, clearly understand "company policy" and the scope of their employment in furthering that policy.

Whether called "children," "young adults," or even "adults," students are inexperienced in many ways. Teachers are presumed to be mature adults who have considerable training and authority. This natural imbalance between faculty members and students closely resembles the definition of a fiduciary relationship, in which one party's power and general competence are considerably less than another's and the weaker party relies heavily on the stronger party. Such a relationship often goes well beyond normal contractual relationships. The law views breaches of this kind of relationship seriously.

Although all teachers doubt their authority over students from time to time, they are a powerful social and intellectual presence in children's lives. In recognition of this fact, many states, at least in their public schools, have very specific laws governing the deportment of teachers, ranging from prohibitions against dating students and strict limits on corporal punishment—if it is allowed at all—to general causes for terminating a teacher's contract for "conduct unbecoming . . . ."

Credentials and evaluation

Beginning with a teacher's own credentials, it is vital for faculty files to be accurate and complete. The head, the academic dean, and department chairmen have not only the authority but the responsibility to check faculty credentials and to keep appropriate files (see Chapter 2, on hiring procedures and employment contracts). This duty should exist as a matter of policy and could well be found to exist as a matter of law. For example, a school's negligent assignment of an unqualified or otherwise incompetent person that results in physical injury to a student is a tort.

The files on a faculty member, which should contain professional employment information and evaluations, should be available only to that person and to that person's supervisors. Supervisors may also have confidential files that they do not share with faculty members themselves. With the authority to keep files, confidential or not, comes the responsibility to keep them out of the public eye and otherwise to use them judiciously.

Faculty members may keep their own files, containing copies of letters of recommendation, citations for excellent performance, evaluations, and the like. They do not, however, have the right to add documents to the files their superiors keep.

When a file contains criticism of a faculty member, presumably it is serious enough to keep—and to cure. It is therefore recommended that criticism of the kind that comes in an evaluation be kept in a teacher's file, on the assumption either that it was serious enough to be in the file in the first place and the teacher is given credit for rectifying it, or that the situation has not been rectified and the person's contract has been terminated. Schools should check federal statutes and those of their state to see how long to keep a teacher's file after termination.

The threat of defamation charges can almost always be obviated by the defense of truth. As with students' files, professional observations in faculty files should be both true and useful, not malicious. Terms like "not our type," "sour," and "lazy" are not useful and are potentially defamatory, in that they are subjective and allow for the possibility of making the teacher the object of ridicule. Information in files is usually the basis for promotions and recommendations for future employment. If this information is negative and untrue, a teacher may be able to show that it is malicious and thus outside of the qualified privilege employers have when making evaluations. In such a case, the faculty member would have a course of action for defamation and loss of future earnings.

Just as evaluations of students' performances must be fair, constructive, and rationally related to the activity being evaluated, so must faculty evaluations. It seems obvious but is nevertheless worth saying that a teacher's employment contract, the tasks the teacher actually performs, and the evaluative criteria applied to that person as a faculty member should absolutely conform one to the other. If, for example, an A student in science has her grade reduced because she will not sweep the laboratory floor, her outrage will match that of the faculty member who is given a poor recommendation as an English teacher because of his reluctance to chaperone off-campus parties. Courts do not become involved in deciding whether a student is a good linguist or whether one teacher is better than another. They do, however, become involved when the plaintiff can show a pattern of repression that is arbitrary, capricious, or discriminatory.

To date, the term "educational malpractice" has not been defined in terms of a cause of action largely because it is too broad and because failure to learn does not necessarily mean failure to teach in the eyes of the court.

All faculty members and administrators must make sure that catalogue descriptions of courses are accurate, that the faculty members assigned to teach particular courses are trained to do so, and that the evaluations of students in those courses are consistent with the stated objectives of the course. The student who enters a school as a girl and graduates as a girl would not have a cause of action because of the school's failure to make her mature, as claimed in the inscription carved over the library door. But that same student, if she had a reading problem, would have a cause of action if the school had contracted to provide a specified number of hours of special help with a qualified and competent reading teacher and had failed to do so and the student's skills did not improve, or if the school intentionally and fraudulently — tort — sent the parents misleading progress reports.

Like students, teachers rely on their supervisors and the institution at large for fair and consistent treatment, for fair and constructive criticism, and for accurate record keeping. An independent school's reputation, and thus its attractiveness in the marketplace, tend to be the strongest controls on the quality of relations between individuals and the school.

Hierarchy of responsibilities

As stated earlier, a faculty member's responsibility is primarily to the institution, then to all students in the school. This responsibility runs to the students as a group and to the protection of their health, safety, and welfare, which is often distressingly at odds with what a teacher thinks and feels when trying to develop a confidential relationship with an individual student. Because most teachers are not skilled mental health professionals, they must, when dealing with a child under a great deal of stress or a child having traits that make him dangerous to himself or others, resist the urge to be a "catcher in the rye." They must face the fact that developing a confidential relationship in cases like these is far less important than protecting the child and those around the child or, in the long run, than helping the child get the appropriate attention.

A dangerous situation can arise when a teacher who is also a student's "adviser" responds alone to the student's crisis rather than recognizing that the problem is serious enough to deserve the attention of people who are specifically trained to deal with it. After the crisis passes a certain point, even the best intentions on the part of the teacher who is attempting to treat it can become increasingly less relevant protection in what might turn out to be a lawsuit against the faculty member and the school for negligence. And a faculty member who knows confidentially that a student is unstable and dangerous and does not report it may be personally liable if that student damages property or injures himself or others.

If a teacher becomes aware of certain outside forces detrimentally at work on a student, he or she has a responsibility to help that student deal with them. In the case of child neglect or child abuse, some states require the teacher to report it to the head of the school, who in turn is required to report it to the appropriate authority or suffer civil penalties. Note that where such statutes exist a teacher's "good faith belief" that the child is being abused is perfect protection against lawsuits by parents for defamation.

Academic freedom

In most independent schools, curriculum development is a matter of collegial cooperation, and teaching in accordance with the curriculum as ultimately designed is a teacher's contractual responsibility. To a degree, however, curriculum content and the choice of texts and books in the library are, though often with great latitude, controlled by forces other than the First Amendment of the United States Constitution. Whereas public school boards may not exercise an individual member's prejudice and personal taste to control what books are placed on the shelves, such choices by teachers and administrators in independent schools are sometimes made in recognition that the independence of the school is a function of the attitudes of those who pay tuition and those who make gifts to the school.

Outside school, in activities not related to employment, a faculty member's expression of beliefs is widely protected. Even though they occur off campus, however, certain gross behaviors may be deemed so "unbecoming a teacher" that the teacher could be terminated for engaging in them.

Classroom and laboratory conditions

A teacher exerts the most direct authority over students in the classroom. Professionalism, as well as contract and tort law, demands that teachers do what they say they are going to do in the classroom and that they exhibit more control over their subject matter and themselves than is expected of students. The qualifications and ability of teachers to teach specific subject matter have been addressed above, under contract and quasi contract theories, in Chapters 2 and 4. Discipline and "due process," issues governed by contract theories and tort theories, are dealt with below, in Chapter 4. Some tort issues are best dealt with here, however.

A professional is expected to know the difference between encouraging and belittling a student in the classroom. A tort action for intentional infliction of emotional distress may follow an outburst by a frustrated teacher who so ridicules and belittles a student in front of other students that the student is not only defamed but is impeded from intellectual and personal growth. If a student suffers physically from that distress, his or her case will be even stronger in court.

Short of self-esteem, and in spite of the Supreme Court's decision that corporal punishment in public schools does not violate the Constitution, hitting students is a tort and in some cases is criminally actionable under state law. Courts assume that teachers are skilled in controlling themselves in classroom settings and do not give much leeway to defenses that might work in other circumstances, such as "fighting words" that lead to a fight between adults in a tavern.

"Assault" means putting a person in immediate fear for his or her own safety, and "battery" means any unauthorized, unconsented-to touching of another person. Of the two, battery holds greater potential for danger because, even within a relatively broad range of socially acceptable touching, the courts look to the expectations of the aggrieved party as well. The coach who swats a male football player on the field in friendly fashion does something that is generally accepted. But the law—and decency—take quite a different view of that same person when he does the same thing to a female student in English class. Courts assume that a professional adult knows the appropriate limits and nature of acceptable physical contact.

More mundane but no less actionable classroom circumstances that could lead to lawsuits involve classroom equipment, including chairs, tables, and any other object that is dangerous or could become dangerous if badly maintained. The most dramatic possibility for this type of liability exists in the science laboratory, where teachers must oversee acids, poisons, and potentially explosive materials with great care. If the school is unable to provide what the prudent professional today would customarily have as protective measures in the laboratory— safety goggles, locked cabinets, emergency showers—the school should not offer courses that require the use of dangerous materials.

In the laboratory, and elsewhere to some degree, teachers are responsible for what students under their supervision do to one another as well as for whatever harm might befall a student working alone. The theories governing these circumstances involve supervisory responsibilities, professional judgment, and teaching skill in that the "level of care" or "duty owed" students is measured by how well teachers prepare students to undertake certain kinds of laboratory activities.

Note also that teachers may be responsible for what students take out of the laboratory. If, for example, acids or explosives hurt someone on the school bus or even at home and can be traced back to the laboratory at school, the school and the teacher may well be held liable for negligence. The legal test would be how reasonably the teacher had acted to prevent such an occurrence.

Under certain circumstances, teachers are responsible not only for what children take from the classroom but for the children themselves when they leave the classroom. No matter how disruptive a child may be, it is vitally important for the school to have procedures for supervising at all times children who are sent out of a class. A child who is disruptive enough to be asked to leave a classroom — or, especially, the school grounds — probably cannot be relied upon to go to the principal's office, study hall, or home alone.

Should such a child be sent from a classroom and leave the school grounds and then be injured, the school might be held responsible. Any time a student is suspended or otherwise sent home during the school day, the parents must be notified and proper arrangements be made for escorting the child from school to home, thereby transferring responsibility from the school to the parent.

Schools have even been held liable for injuries to children not their students who came onto the campus uninvited during school hours, were disruptive and sent off, and then were injured. Liability in these situations is established after considering all of the circumstances of the incident, including the child's age, maturity, and physical and mental health. Similarly, if a child is injured or becomes ill at school, the child should be attended by an adult until the parents are notified and arrive or, if necessary, a doctor or ambulance comes.

Enrichment

Good teachers commonly look for ways to enrich their courses and programs through state assistance, inexpensive alternatives to substantial purchases, and off-campus activities.

In the case of state aid, the Supreme Court has held that state aid to independent schools must meet a three-part test of having secular purpose, of neither inhibiting nor advancing religion, and of not leading to excessive entanglement between the state and the private enterprise. Recent application of this test has severely restricted state aid for textbooks and supplements, certain services, such as tests and test administrators, and certain other activities required of independent schools by states that then absorb the cost of the requirement. Any aid that could at a school's choice be turned to sectarian purposes, such as field trips, is not allowed.

Tax money to aid independent schools is a subject of debate in Congress. It is enough to say here that allowing tuition tax credits, plus a state's monitoring of independent schools under its police powers, plus providing transportation for independent school students, plus certain textbooks and testing do not, even taken together, successfully raise the issue of "state action." That is because the state's contribution and control do not—yet—sufficiently rob the school of its independence and effectively make it an agent of the state.

Even with a degree of outside aid, finances remain tight for independent schools. One relatively inexpensive way for classroom teachers to reduce costs is to photocopy materials rather than requiring the school or students to buy their own. But schools should be aware that photocopying is governed—ambiguously, to be sure—by what is known as the "fair use doctrine" reflected in the 1976 Copyright Law. Whether copied materials violate this doctrine is tested by such points as the purpose for which copies are made, the nature of the work copied, the amount of the work copied, and the potential impact on the publisher's market.

Although field trips and other off-campus activities are dealt with in more detail in the section on volunteers, in Chapter 8, faculty members who are involved are clearly responsible for prudence and due diligence in planning and supervision, whether serving as chaperones of off-campus parties or supervisors on field trips. Any off-campus activity on which the school places its stamp of approval—especially one involving faculty members—offers potential legal exposure for the institution and for its agents personally. Here, as elsewhere, appropriate insurance coverage for teachers and volunteers is very important. An obvious example is carefully considered insurance coverage for faculty members or volunteers driving school vehicles or their own on school business.

4.

Students and Due Process

The Fifth Amendment of the United States Constitution was made applicable to the states by the Fourteenth Amendment. Both amendments use the words "due process of law," and the Fourteenth Amendment uses "equal protection of the laws." The Constitution protects individuals from actions of the state. In the absence of finding a "state action," these two amendments do not apply to the way independent schools deal with people, but the *concepts* may. For schools, the major concept is "fundamental fairness."

The courts, not peopled by professional educators, are loath to become involved in the discretionary judgments made by educators. When they do become involved, courts approach the educational issues before them by using analogies to frame the issues in a way that is comprehensible to them. Thus language such as "due process" and "equal protection" is inevitably used, even though it does not apply in its strictest sense.

"Equal protection" means that people who are similarly situated must be treated similarly. "Due process" means that, given a particular right — or, in some cases, privilege — the procedural fairness necessary to protect that right must be considered. In both instances, "fundamental fairness" is a critical concept that serves as a guiding light in the evaluation of actions involving independent schools in contract, quasi contract, and even tort law, even though no state action is present.

To determine what students' rights, including reasonable expectations, are, and what procedures are due in the protection of those rights, a court looks at all of the representations made by a defendant school in its catalogues, bulletins, rules and regulations, course descriptions, development brochures, and verbally by the school's agents. The reason for this type of inquiry is that actions against independent schools are rarely constitutional in nature. More typically, they are based in contract and tort law, and so a court will try to determine the basis of the contractual relationship between the school and its students.

Contract and quasi contract issues

A public high school that allows one religious denomination but not another to meet on its campus could be assailed on two grounds: first, equal protection — denial of freedom of religious expression to one group while allowing another, similarly situated group to enjoy the same — and second, separation of church and state — the unconstitutionality of a public school becoming involved with any activity that is not secular in nature and that enhances or inhibits freedom of religion.

In a typical independent school, this situation could not be successfully attacked on constitutional grounds. It could, however, be challenged on contractual grounds under certain circumstances. For example, if the school's catalogue advertised a commitment to nourish each student's sectarian beliefs, the school would be in the wrong to select among established religions. The families deprived would argue that, even though the school's commitment was not within the "four corners" of the written enrollment contract, they had relied on the school's representation in making their "bargain." As in other situations, a school must provide what it advertises.

The requirement that a school do what it says it is going to do is, of course, not limited to providing certain facilities and programs; it includes a student's reliance on a school's advertised disciplinary procedures, which, to whatever degree they are spelled out in writing, must be adhered to scrupulously lest a school's actions be attacked as arbitrary and capricious violations of the process due a student under his or her contractual relationship with the school.

Schools may, and some do, attempt to protect their discretion simply by stating in their catalogue, in quite general terms, that a student may be expelled for some broad reason: "If, at the discretion of the academy, it is deemed that a student is no longer able to act in a manner consistent with the academy's traditions . . ." Such phrasing gives the school enormous discretion but does not provide perfect protection against students' claims. Because of the obvious opportunity for arbitrary and capricious abuse of the school's discretion, courts look carefully at the exercise of such discretion. A court would look to how the school had treated other students in similar circumstances to establish its own notion of the real criteria on which discretionary decisions had been made and then apply those criteria to the case in question.

The foregoing deals, in part, with what is known as "cause" for disciplinary action. A school should also have a statement of what type of "notice" is given to students and their parents or guardians before any action is taken against a student either for academic performance or deportment. Finally, for both legal and sound policy reasons, a school should also indicate the process it uses for determination once allegations have been made against a student.

Tort liability

Chapter 3, on the faculty, deals with common situations of tort liability for the school and for individual teachers. In the case of teachers, tort liability arises from negligence that leads to injury as a result of a teacher's unreasonableness — imprudent or unwise action — or incomplete or otherwise improper following of procedures. In such an instance, the plaintiff's complaint would inevitably show "counts" (distinct charges) of tort and breach of contract. These counts would sound fundamentally the same, for both would be based on the plaintiff's reasonable expectations and defendant's actions.

Public school situations involving search and seizure, controlled by the Fourth Amendment of the Constitution and, in many states, by applicable statutes, can lead to lawsuits based on alleged violations of students' expectations of privacy of their persons and of their lockers or dormitory rooms. In most states, searches of students require "reasonable suspicion" on the part of the faculty and administration. However, because of abuses of this subjective standard in public schools, states are increasingly passing statutes that require "probable cause," a standard that is generally applied to all citizens under these circumstances. In practice, the greater the intrusion into the student's privacy the more stringent should be the standard the school applies. For example, using specially trained dogs to sniff out drugs might be permissible under the "reasonable suspicion" standard, but a strip search of students is not permissible under the same standard.

The "in loco parentis" doctrine is being diluted by litigation. In independent boarding schools, even though they describe themselves as having a "family atmosphere," faculty searches of dormitory rooms may begin to fall outside this doctrine and be encompassed by measures based on a student's expectation of privacy, which in turn would be based on how the school, with specificity, described student housing and the privacy therein. Further, consistent with the sliding scale of suspicion required, the search of a student's room is less intrusive than a search of a locked trunk inside that room.

Recalling discussions of "state action," it is important to note that private schools on their own operate according to a standard different from that required once they are cooperating with state or local police. Police are required to show probable cause and to obtain a warrant to search a person's room. The police cannot circumvent these constitutional requirements simply by instructing private school employees to carry out a search for them. Evidence presented to the police by the school under such circumstances is not admissible in court because it has been unconstitutionally obtained. The school can, however, use the evidence in its own disciplinary procedures, provided it stays within what it advertises as its methods of investigation. On the other hand, if the police legitimately gain evidence — drugs, weapons — on or off the campus, the school can use this evidence in dealing with the student or students possessing it.

Suspension and expulsion

The legal theories that generally apply to wrongful suspension, expulsion, or both are typically breach of contract, intentional infliction of emotional distress, defamation, loss of future earnings, and possibly personal injury. The first three theories are applicable when a school's publicized process either has not been followed or has been followed haphazardly. For example, a school that publishes prudent standards of "reasonable suspicion" of cause of an infraction, notice of allegations to the student, and provisions for a hearing could be liable in breach of contract or in tort if a student who is "known to be troublesome" is summarily expelled without the protection of the published process. In this case, the student can also claim that she has been "picked on and made miserable," that she has been unfairly labeled as, say, "a drug user," and that her expulsion deprives her of an education at a school that is particularly appropriate for her growth and thereby interferes with her future capacity to earn a living.

As with employee evaluations, a school is privileged to speak openly about students. This privilege and the defense of truth may both disappear, however, in a case charging defamation where malice can be shown — that the school has publicly and repeatedly bludgeoned a student with an obnoxious truth in such a way as to be "shocking to the conscience."

In extraordinary cases involving "clear and present danger," procedures for hearings can be invoked after a student has been suspended. Obvious examples are students who are intoxicated or "stoned" on drugs, who possess weapons, or who are otherwise immediately dangerous to themselves and others.

As indicated earlier, courts are extremely reluctant to substitute their judgment for the judgment of educators in cases involving educational issues. In the case of suspensions, for example, the court would focus on the length of a suspension only in relation to the process due the student to make a fundamentally fair determination of his or her case. The more severe the punishment the more elaborate the process due.

As a matter of policy, punishments ought to bear some rational relation to offenses. At some point, for example, a lengthy suspension is really an expulsion, for all practical purposes; a three-week suspension equals almost 10 per cent of a school year of 160 + days. Thus if a school considers cutting one class a serious offense because "each class is important," then depriving a student of weeks of classes ought to be triggered only by the most serious offenses.

When suspension is the outcome of a nondangerous situation, the school must be meticulous in notifying parents and holding a prompt hearing. A dangerous situation — possession of a weapon — can be dealt with by suspending the student immediately and having a hearing later. It is vital for schools to recognize that in a dangerous case their responsibility goes beyond simply removing a student from school and scheduling a hearing at a later date. Schools are responsible for students during the school day under most circumstances, of which this is one. The school is therefore responsible for supervising the suspended student until that student is delivered over to the family. For example, a family might well sue a school that sends a child off the campus during the day, for whatever reason, who is injured on the way home. The parents would charge the school with failing in its duty to supervise.

Under contract and tort law, expulsion requires cause, notice, and some type of hearing or review. Even though the same types of behavior that can lead to suspension can also lead to expulsion, the degree of scrutiny and attention to agreed-upon procedures is expected to be higher because the result is permanent. A student disciplinary committee's recommendation for suspension might be appropriate if the suspension is brief and other procedures are met, but a school head would be foolish to allow the same committee to effect an expulsion. In fact, school heads have the responsibility to review all recommendations for suspension and expulsion. This is true not only for all the obvious reasons but also because not to do so is improper delegation of the faculty's and administration's authority and in all probability is not bargained for or in any way expected by families who entrust their children to a school.

What happens after suspension? The student should be brought back into school in good faith. It is intentional infliction of emotional distress if the student is allowed to return and then is constantly taunted by reminders of past conduct. Further, the school should consider having a stated policy setting a "statute of limitations" that governs how long a suspension stays on a student's record, for a court might view it as "fundamentally unfair" for a senior to be expelled for a second major offense if the first one occurred in the freshman year.

As schools well know, expulsion rarely ends a school's relationship with a student. Expulsion, one of the hardest actions a school ever has to take, is imposed only after agonizing evaluations of a student's past conduct and potential future placement. Once these evaluations lead to the conclusion that a student should be expelled, the action should be taken in good faith, not as retribution. In most cases, the school continues to work with the student and his or her family to find counseling and other help for the student in a new setting. This is not legally required, but the absence of good-faith dealings on the part of the school can lead to litigation if the school is unwilling to forward records—unless tuition has not been paid—or the school passes on an angry and otherwise unprofessional report of what the student has or has not done to deserve expulsion, which could be viewed as defamation.

Speaking of a disciplined student in glowing terms does not necessarily protect the school, either. The next school the student attends may have a claim against the expelling school for misrepresenting the student in such a way that, except for the misrepresentation, the next school would not have taken the student or, in the case of public school districts, would have classified the student differently.

Student activities

A student's participation in the life of the school is a matter of school tradition and obligation under contract or quasi contract. Beyond that, a student has no legally sufficient basis for challenges to the school. A student has no protected right to be involved in the school's newspaper or glee club.

The adults in a school bear the most responsibility. For this reason, though clearly not for this reason alone, adults must retain ultimate authority. This is true in areas of delegation — when students serve on a discipline committee, for example — and in matters of censorship, for not only can faculty members censor school publications, they must do so to protect the institution against libel suits.

Protecting students against "bad taste" is very different for independent schools than it is in public schools. First Amendment guarantees do not extend to nonstate schools, and so private school employees may exert their taste — and many parents expect them to — in school publications and even in the choice of library books, which has been the subject of vigorous public school litigation for some time. And, as one might imagine, these lawsuits are often interesting scrutinies of the difference between matters of subjective "taste" as such and the use of "taste" to chill political or racial beliefs unpopular with a local school committee.

5.

Coaches
and Athletics

Whereas psychological and intellectual damage are hard to assess, physical injury is tangible. Skillful protection against injury to student athletes takes training, knowledge, and expense. These are absolutely necessary, however, to protect the school and possibly the individual teacher-coach against liability. Even if a student is insured against injury, an insurance company may decide to recover its payments from the coach and the school under certain circumstances; this is known as subrogation of a claim. Thus, for example, a soccer coach's skills must transcend the ability to shout "Don't bunch up" at a group of players on the field.

Most independent schools are proud that their teachers know students in and out of the classroom. Much of their nonacademic time together is spent on athletic fields, where teachers also coach. The athletic director and full-time athletic staff are most immediately responsible for assessing and developing the skills of other teacher-coaches. That these coaches actually teach students how to play games is a matter of contractual duty in most schools because most schools advertise an athletic program. That they instruct under reasonably safe conditions is a matter of tort law. For these reasons, the athletic director and the teacher-coaches should insist that they be given proper instruction to equip them to fulfill those duties that go beyond mere supervision. The deportment of a teacher-coach is measured in court by what teacher-coaches customarily do in this role, even though an individual defendant's personal liability might be mitigated by his or her particular credentials.

Obviously a coach is required to know the rules of the game and ought to know drills that are appropriate not only to conditioning students for a particular sport but also to conditioning children of a particular age and maturity. Injuries often occur because of incorrectly chosen warmup exercises and calisthenics, not just because of insufficient ones.

The athletic director, at least, should be required to stay abreast of developments in sports medicine, through reading, workshops, and clinics around the country, and to pass these on to teacher-coaches.

Students' medical records

A school should always require complete medical records of all students and see that they are brought up to date each year. As most school people know, these records contain information about allergies, immunizations, histories of diseases, bone fractures, internal vulnerabilities, and other such details.

As school people also know, parents often wait until they return from summer vacation to ask busy physicians to try to squeeze in the required physical examination. Football season may begin while the school is waiting for the doctor's report, but the school should never allow a student to take part in sports until the physical examination has been completed and the report received. Otherwise, the school could be held negligent for unnecessarily exposing a student to harm.

For example, while asthma attacks and epileptic seizures can occur in the classroom without causing undue alarm, they can be more serious and dangerous on an athletic field, even if the required emergency vehicle is present to take students to the hospital. Also, pre-existing injuries, if negligently aggravated, usually serve only to mitigate damages in a lawsuit by the injured.

An even more delicate situation occurs when a student athlete is injured during practice or a game and the seriousness of the injury is not immediately apparent. In striving to "build character" and win, coaches are often heard to tell athletes to "shake it off" before putting them back into a game. Whether an athlete goes in, stays in, or returns to a game is a coach's responsibility. If a student insists on returning even though he has a headache from a recent tackle, the coach is expected to exercise reasonable judgment that transcends the athlete's eagerness and everyone else's desire to win, and not just be gratified at the athlete's devotion to sport.

A student with an obvious head injury should be removed to a hospital immediately and should not be allowed back on the playing field even for practice until proper professional clearances have been given. Especially under game conditions, emotions and peer pressures — and often parental pressures — run high, but the coach, presumably being the most experienced person in such circumstances, has the duty to rise above these pressures and exercise due care in protecting the safety of the individual.

A coach must therefore be continuously alert to each student's well-being. If an athlete complains, the coach's first response should be one of respect rather than chiding. The coach who forces an overweight fifth grader who complains about a knee onto the trampoline because he or she thinks the student is being a sissy is negligent. If the student's knee gives way while on the trampoline and the student crashes to the floor and is hurt, even the proper placement of the required mats does not protect the coach from liability for negligence in this case.

Playing areas and equipment

When a hockey puck goes through a hockey helmet or when a football helmet splits on impact, the injured party almost always sues the manufacturer of the equipment because the manufacturer has the "deepest pocket" — the ability to pay substantial damage awards — and is probably liable under a range of tort theories involving design and defects. Even so, the coaches, the school, and the trustees can also expect to be defendants after such an injury on the basis that the equipment was ill chosen, improperly fitted, or improperly maintained by the school.

If a coach is not skilled enough to recondition or even maintain equipment, a qualified independent contractor should perform these tasks. Improper in-house maintenance of equipment or trying to make important equipment "last one more year" is false economy when contrasted with the possibility of injury, not to mention the high costs of litigation and damage.

Playing areas themselves represent potential dangers. If the available playing area is inappropriate to a given activity, then the activity must be foregone, no matter how attractive it seems. Injuries that result from diving into a half-empty pool or sliding across glass and stone on the way to first base are obvious examples. Others are allowing wrestlers to work out in confined spaces with unpadded walls, or in steam rooms where they could easily faint and fall, and allowing children to play running games in gymnasiums that have glass doors.

"Due diligence and care" and "custom" are typically the standards against which potential liability is measured in the case of athletic injury. For example, if a wrestler "takes down" another wrestler and breaks his neck on the gymnasium floor next to the central mat, the school could be liable for not having the "customary" peripheral mats in place to give protection. If the peripheral mats are there and the wrestlers go off them and hit the floor, the school may not be found liable for negligence. Examples are easy to cite; the issue is for the adults in charge to take reasonable actions to prevent foreseeable accidents.

One final and not so obvious example is injury that results from overaggressive play. A soccer player consents to a generally accepted degree of physical contact and has no cause of action, such as battery, if an injury results from that contact. The same soccer player does not consent to being kicked in the head on purpose while lying on the ground. In many states, parents are accountable for minors' intentional torts, up to certain monetary limits. Such statutes do not, however, obviate the responsibility of a coach, and thus of the coach's school, if the injured party can show not only that he or she was kicked in the head on purpose but also that the overzealousness of the coach and the general atmosphere and attitude of the school are such that one could have expected the defendant to be mean and aggressive and kick another player in the head.

Eligibility

Except for any contractual responsibility that develops between the student, and the student's family, and the school concerning the student's participation in athletics, no student has a protected right to be on any particular team, let alone to play on any varsity team. The school should spell out in its handbook the criteria for required athletics and the possibility of playing on a team in interscholastic competition. These criteria should include loss of eligibility for disciplinary or academic reasons, and all criteria should be followed.

Title IX of the Education Amendments of 1972 prohibits discrimination on the basis of sex under any "education program or activity receiving federal financial assistance." Even though the majority of independent schools are not affected by this statute, it is increasingly assumed that coeducational schools will make equal, but not necessarily identical, provisions for athletics for students of both sexes. Because states have passed their own laws on this subject, a school's compliance with nondiscriminatory practices may not be legally dependent on receiving federal assistance. As in other areas of the program, a school's offerings of coeducational and single-sex athletic teams should be "as advertised."

Schools themselves can have eligibility problems when it comes to their desire to join certain leagues. It has been settled in case law that a school has neither a "property" nor a "liberty" interest to participate in any particular league, public or private. League participation is a matter of league policy and whatever contractual arrangements may be made between the league and given schools.

6.

The Admission Office

Anyone who is involved in marketing and public relations understands that success depends largely on public knowledge of a product. In schools, the curriculum and extracurricular program are the "products," not the students. Many people decide to send their children to a particular school on the basis of how these products are represented.

Parents often rely heavily on what a school communicates in writing, as well as in conversation, about its programs because few of them are in a position to evaluate professionally what the school has to offer. Thus even when parents visit the school themselves, "caveat emptor" provides a weak defense against a contract action brought by those parents if the school turns out not to be what it says it is.

Note the contrast between parents' reliance on what they see and hear about the school and the school's reliance on what it sees and hears about applicants. Clearly, the school's employees are expected to be professional and have skill and experience in evaluating applicants. Parents have a right to expect that their child, if admitted, has been deemed by professionals to have at least the capacity to survive academically and socially.

Representations to the public

As stated earlier, any representations to the public made by agents of the school who have or who appear to have the authority to make such representations may become part of at least a quasi contractual relationship between the institution and those persons who rely on such representations.

The most obvious body of representations lies in the school's catalogue. Schools are generally proud of themselves and their traditions, and their catalogues reflect this pride. To the extent that a school advertises "quality education" in general terms, this might be regarded as the truth or, at worst, mere puffery. Wherever the catalogue speaks explicitly about program, faculty qualifications, or plant and equipment, however, the school must in fact provide what it advertises.

If the school does not provide what it says it will — "the most sophisticated computer instruction," "Ph.D. instructors at the freshman level," "specially trained teachers of students having reading disabilities" — disappointed consumers, and donors, will point to the catalogue in their suits against the school for breach of contract, saying that they relied, paid, or gave, and the school failed to perform. In the same vein, if the school's catalogue shows a lovely library that in fact is the town library, the catalogue must say so; a proposed new science building must be advertised as such, not as a functioning unit.

Catalogues often contain course descriptions. The school must offer the courses it advertises, making reasonable allowance for curricular modifications during the school year. A possible course may be included in the catalogue but should be described as such; "Music — Independent Study" should be spelled out so that parents are not falsely led to believe that a member of the nearby symphony orchestra will make regular trips to the campus to give their child piano lessons at no extra cost.

Oral representations about the school by its agents also comprise a quasi contract. As a matter of policy, an admission office must train its staff members to control their enthusiasm. In turn, the staff must carefully train any volunteers, such as graduates around the country who are enlisted to recruit for the school, because they may appear to have the authority to make reliable representations about the school. Editing a catalogue or brochure and training staff members and volunteers are well worth the costs involved when compared to potentially bad public relations or the actual expense of a lawsuit.

Admission criteria

Admission officers are busy people, but it makes good sense

for them to take time to work with the faculty, and especially with the curriculum committee, to understand fully what their school offers and to help the faculty develop a realistic understanding of the talents of applicants. With this in mind, the admission office should develop rational criteria for admission to bring into the school students who can benefit from and contribute to it.

Children may have the right to public schooling in their states, but they have no right to attend a particular private school. Nevertheless, in cases of racial discrimination in private, tax-exempt schools, the result of litigation could be money damages, loss of a school's tax-exempt status, *and* admission of the applicants involved. Note that if a school has an affirmative action statement, beyond its statement of non-discriminatory practices, this too should be expressed in its catalogue. A school's membership in an association such as NAIS, which has a strong affirmative action policy, should also be noted.

Application forms are often the first step toward matching student and school. The school may ask anything it wishes on the form, but the governing rationale must be, "Is this question necessary?" Clearly, questions on the admission application must be rationally related to admission criteria, which in turn are rationally related to the school's goals and resources. Such a form can even request photographs for identification, information about physical handicaps, and questions about police records, religion, and parents' marital status and educational backgrounds, as well as the usual academic and personal-interest inventories. The obvious reasons for such questions are that the school must be physically accessible to the students it admits, the school's program must be able to serve its students, and schools do not want students whose behaviorial pathology would stretch the faculty beyond their skills to protect the personal safety and the safety of the property of others and expose the school to lawsuits. Just as there are bona fide occupational qualifications for employment, so are there legitimate — if sometimes obnoxious — qualifying attributes for admission. If a school gives preference to current students' brothers and sisters or to children of graduates, that preference should be disclosed in the catalogue and elsewhere.

Most schools charge a fee for processing applications. This fee should be reasonably related to the actual cost of doing so. A high fee could be challenged by the family whose child is turned down and who believe that the child's application was treated superficially. On the other hand, if a school's admission office is large enough, it might want to consider charging more and providing more, functioning more or less as a placement counselor for students not admitted.

Whatever the admission process may be, it should be advertised and adhered to. Statements about the process must make clear that it is designed to protect the student and the school. Just as schools may misrepresent themselves, so may applicants; a careful review of each applicant's credentials is therefore vital. If, for example, a foreign student not available for an interview states that she is able to read and speak English fluently, the school would be on solid ground to keep her deposit or first-semester tuition if it discovered that she had misrepresented herself and the school could not serve her — assuming, of course, that the school never represented itself as a bilingual, bicultural institution able to serve her.

Although the Buckley Amendment — the federal Family Educational Rights and Privacy Act — does not apply to the vast majority of independent schools, its guidelines are simple and fair and are recommended. Schools should disclose to parents that any and all information about students may be sent forward to colleges to which the student applies and back to other schools from which students have come. Further, the people writing recommendations should know in advance to whom the school might show these recommendations.

The only other form requested of all students is the medical form. Certain people in the school should know what information this form contains. The school nurse and doctor should know if a given student needs to have special medication available at all times; the athletic department should be aware of physical problems; and the teaching faculty should know about visual and auditory deficiencies. Parents' authorization for hospitalization and emergency surgery should be included in this form.

Financial aid

If financial aid is available, the procedure for awarding it, and its sources, should be publicized. Although schools have enormous discretion in awarding financial aid, they could come under fire, particularly in the area of charges of racial discrimination.

Most independent schools use the School Scholarship Service's forms and processing plus parents' federal income tax returns. If families are unwilling to provide this information when asked for it, they then forego consideration for financial aid. The questions on the School Scholarship Service's form are rationally related to the specific purpose for which they are asked: responsible decisions about financial aid cannot be made without this information.

Whether a school "invests" in a student is a difficult decision, at least because of its reputation and a student's future, but two additional factors can complicate the process: divorced parents, and overcommitment of resources by the school. In the latter case, the business and admission offices must work closely together to see to it that the school does not offer financial aid to students for whom it does not have the money. If this does happen, these students, once admitted, have a contractual right to attend the school, which must either find additional resources or simply take a loss.

In the case of divorced parents, difficulty may arise when the custodial parent has little money and the noncustodial parent's responsibilities are defined—and being met—by law under the divorce decree. How a school handles such situations must be carefully spelled out. Schools must be wary of a problem that may arise: tuition payments are not tax-deductible. Thus a noncustodial parent may not make a payment in lieu of tuition and attempt to write it off as a gift to the school. To do so not only jeopardizes this parent's position as a taxpayer who might be made to pay penalties and interest; it could also lead to the school's loss of its tax-exempt status.

The noncustodial parent of a student receiving financial aid may make a gift to the school and take a tax deduction for the gift, but the line between this gift and the child's financial aid must be kept very clear. In many cases this line vanishes because some schools have a policy of *asking* the noncustodial parent to pay tuition, or even of asking a child's grandparents to pay tuition. Arguably, once this request has been made, has been refused, the child has been awarded financial aid, and then the person previously approached makes a gift, that gift could be challenged by the Internal Revenue Service.

Another form of financial assistance is "sliding scale tuitions." The issue here is political. Legal issues, if they arise at all, usually stem from improper publicity or procedures and failure to adhere to publicized procedures, which could lead to inequitable distribution of the tuition burden among similarly situated families.

Student loan programs

Thanks to generous and sophisticated donors, student loan programs are becoming a significant part of the financial aid programs of many schools. The issues for a school are to understand the details of a donor's intent to publicize and to adhere strictly to loan policies, especially in the area of disclosure, and to collect loan repayments.

Before accepting gifts for loans, a school should carefully examine the conditions a donor sets to make sure that the school wishes and is able to meet these conditions and impose them on others. The procedures prescribed by the donor must be followed, if the school accepts the gift; otherwise, the donor may withdraw it. If, for example, a donor prescribed only certain uses for unused funds and found that they were being applied to activities beyond the terms of the gift—even though they were legal and important activities—the donor could cancel for breach of contract. In this situation, the school itself would have to assume the burden of carrying those students with whom loan contracts had already been drawn.

Presumably, eligibility for a loan is determined by using standard admission criteria and the procedures of the School Scholarship Service. Again, fair and clear policies diligently followed will protect the school. The institution sets the policies, but its attorney should review all documents, including the loan agreement and the disclosure statement.

Student loans, like any others, are expressly contractual in nature. They are collectible, provided the school has performed its part of the contract. When a loan falls due, either on schedule or prematurely because of expulsion or withdrawal, collection may become an issue. If the school has trouble collecting, it should consult its attorney for general advice and to ask about using a reputable collection agency.

7.

The Business Office

Depending on the size of a school, its business office may be a substantial department within the institution or it may simply be a couple of drawers in the head's desk. Either way, the business manager must exercise due diligence and care and is accountable for the "reasonable" getting and dispensing of school funds. Legally, this reasonableness is based on "custom in business practices" and is governed by state and federal laws that require certain procedures for recording and reporting by nonprofit institutions.

The trustees approve the budget, and it is the responsibility of the business office to adhere to it. Who sets the internal policies of the business office is a question that should be answered explicitly by the trustees, head, and business manager. Unclear policies in this area could lead to confusion having adverse legal ramifications.

Tuition and financial aid

Tuition is usually the major source of general operating income in a school. Parents expect to be billed accurately and on schedule and expect to have their money spent only in ways that directly benefit their children. Parents can reasonably expect tuition income to be used for certain other purposes, such as financial aid, but this should be publicized specifically because not all parents are altruistic and would like to weigh such commitments in advance of enrolling their child.

Not all parents pay tuition on time. Business office policies governing late payments should conform closely to the policies of the entire institution, which should have a consistent, publicized policy about visiting any of the sins of parents upon their children. If a student is not allowed to enter school the following semester if tuition is not paid by a certain date, everyone should know that policy and expect it to be followed.

Tuition refund and retention policies should also be spelled out clearly in the school's enrollment contract for parents who have paid their tuition and whose children withdraw or are expelled. In a time when tuition refund insurance is so common, a business office might be considered negligent for not telling parents that this type of insurance is available and the names of firms offering it. In the case of expulsion, the school need not refund tuition unless it has failed in some other contractual obligation to the student. The school may need this money because it is often impossible to make up the loss by admitting another student in the middle of the year to take over tuition payments—a student who is capable of meeting the school's admission requirements and entering a new social and academically competitive setting after the school year is under way.

A school has the legal right to collect tuition that is in arrears and may go to court if necessary. If a school has a policy of withholding formal records and the diploma until tuition is paid, this policy should also be included in the enrollment contract. State consumer protection laws protect against harsh collection practices; it is unlikely, however, that an independent school would resort to these tactics even without such laws. It is more likely that political considerations prevail over legal issues in deliberations on how to proceed against parents who do not pay. If a collection agency is hired, this should be done on the advice of the school's attorney.

As indicated in Chapter 6, the business and admission offices should stay in close touch about all matters pertaining to admission and financial aid. The business office needs to know the school's enrollment capacity and the potential for reaching that capacity from year to year; the admission office must know that underadmitting and overadmitting each have direct financial consequences; and both departments should clearly understand that a student, once admitted, has a legal right to attend whether he or she pays full tuition or receives financial aid.

Fund management

Once money is allocated for a particular purpose, the intended users of that money rely on its being available and act accordingly. For a school's science department to borrow funds earmarked for that school's mathematics department is not illegal, but it is not good fiscal practice. If the science department contracts with an outside firm to supply laboratory equipment and relies on those same funds, however, a cause of action on behalf of an outside third party can arise. Both examples are cases of interfund borrowing, which reflects poor communication and planning and is potentially dangerous in any case.

A school's donors also rely on it to carry out the purposes of their gifts as stated. Donors have cause to revoke their gifts if these gifts are not directed to the fund or department originally specified. Even a potential donor may rescind a pledge if he or she discovers that gifts are not strictly kept in and dispensed from the categories specified by donors.

Boards of trustees often delegate management of endowment funds to an independent contractor that handles investments. In such a case, the trustees and the business office still have ultimate responsibility for assuring donors and others that funds are being prudently managed — "prudence" here meaning that funds are not being placed in unduly risky investments or being wasted by being held in investments that show consistently poor performance.

A school should be wary of accepting a gift in the form of stock from the donor's own corporation, especially if closely held, that the donor asks the school not to sell. The donor must have the present intent to give, the recipient must have the present intent to receive, and the donor must relinquish all dominion and control over the gift. If these conditions are not met, both the donor's tax deduction and the school's tax-exempt status could be in jeopardy.

What if a donor's restrictions on a gift become illegal or otherwise impossible for the institution to meet? Some states subscribe to the "cy-pres" doctrine, which says that a recipient may go to ask a court in equity to recognize a change in circumstances and allow the recipient to modify the restrictions on the gift to correspond to current realities in society.

Unrelated business income

Beyond tuition and endowment is at least one other form of

income: unrelated business income. Such income results from enterprises that are not directly related to the educational purpose for which the institution was granted tax-exempt status by the Internal Revenue Service.

To date, such enterprises as an on-campus bookstore and a skate exchange have not been deemed "unrelated," but income from leasing school premises to outsiders has. Nonexempt activities must be "substantial," and not "incidental," to threaten the tax-exempt status of the "parent" organization. An activity is not unrelated if it has a direct primary relation to the institution's primary business, education. Determinations are based almost solely on the facts of an individual case. The school should check with its counsel to see how such income should be reported and whether taxes should be paid. Income is income; serious problems can arise from not reporting it properly.

Government regulations

Certain types of federal and state assistance (see "state action" in the Glossary) provide income yet cause private schools to meet standards they otherwise would not have to meet. Numerous other state and federal statutes apply regardless of federal funding, however. Three such statutes should be mentioned here.

Title VII of the Civil Rights Act of 1964, amended through the Equal Employment Opportunity Act in 1972 to include educational institutions, prohibits employers from discrimination in hiring, discharging, or otherwise adversely affecting the status of an employee or classifying among employees on the basis of race, color, religion, sex, or national origin.

The Civil Rights Act 42 U.S.C. Section 1981 says that "all persons . . . shall have the same right in every state . . . to make and enforce contracts . . . and to the full and equal benefit of all laws and proceedings for the security of persons and property as is enjoyed by white citizens."

The Age Discrimination in Employment Act, as its name implies, prohibits employers from discriminating in personnel practices on the basis of age.

Following are three examples of statutes under which standards affect only those schools that receive federal funding — and arguably only in those areas to which funds are applied — but two federal district courts have recently differed on the issue of whether such funding is "program specific" or "institution wide."

The Family Educational Rights and Privacy Act, or Buckley Amendment, one of the Education Amendments of 1974, applies also if *students* receive federal funds through certain programs.

The Rehabilitation Act of 1973 protects the rights of handicapped persons to participate in federally funded programs.

Title IX of the Education Amendments of 1972 prohibits discrimination on the basis of sex in any educational program receiving federal financial assistance.

Here, as elsewhere, many schools have elected to observe the spirit of these statutes as a matter of policy.

Contracts for goods and services

All contracts should be reviewed by the school's attorney to make sure, in advance, what specific remedies exist in case of breach. Contracts are valuable to both parties because they require, or ought to require, careful initial negotiation and ultimately determine the parties' rights if the terms of a contract cannot be met.

Contracts for the purchase of goods, such as laboratory equipment and textbooks, should contain an express statement that "time is of the essence." When a contract is written, it is not unusual for the parties to estimate the cost to each of them in the event of breach and to include these costs as "liquidated damages." The amount of such damages should take into account the costs of renting the same type of equipment until the original vendor or a new one can provide the equipment bargained for. When considering purchases of goods or services from members of the school community or their firms, the school must be especially careful. See Chapter 1 on conflict of interest.

Contracts for personal services, especially teachers' contracts, as described in Chapter 2, should be clear. Wages, hours, specific duties, and the end point of staff contracts should be carefully spelled out, as should causes and procedures for termination.

Maintenance

Even though depreciation is generally not a useful item on the income independent schools report on IRS Form 990, keeping an actual fund for depreciation does have a definite purpose. Expenses of depreciation are real, inevitable, and in some cases might be required, directly or indirectly, by the federal Occupational Health and Safety Act or by state and local laws controlling health and safety aspects of the institution.

A school is always potentially liable in tort for negligently maintained buildings and grounds where students or visitors or, in many cases, even trespassers may be injured by a defect about which the property owner knows or should know and correct. Further, a school is liable for supervising its buildings and grounds and for providing responsible forms of security, such as smoke detectors and night watchmen to protect persons and property.

Employment and employees

Beyond the normal concerns involving buildings and grounds employees are two that deserve special mention: aliens and child labor. Title VII of the Civil Rights Act of 1964 provides that people may not be discriminated against in employment on the grounds of national origin—in this case, "alienage"—and that aliens must be paid at the same rate as other employees, once they have shown the papers required for employment in the United States.

The issue of child labor is important because the line between using students for the school's benefit—student labor—and having students engage in work for an educational purpose—in a "work program"—can be very thin. Child labor is governed by the Commerce Clause of the U.S. Constitution and has been regulated since 1938 under the Fair Labor Standards Act. For most jobs, the minimum age is sixteen, and the minimum wage is the same as that for adults unless specific allowance is granted for paying 85 per cent of adult wages. Whereas waiting on tables without compensation might be a tradition having an educational purpose for students at a school, painting the gymnasium is quite arguably a task that specifically and only benefits the school.

Violations of child labor laws currently trigger fines of $1,000 per violation and $10,000 or six months in jail for willful violations.

Worker's compensation applies to injuries suffered in the course of performing duties of employment. As in on-the-job injuries in which workers are covered by worker's compensation, in child labor cases there is also no contributory negligence: the degree to which the child is negligent does not mitigate damages.

The interesting aspect of worker's compensation is the court's willingness to extend the definition of duties to cover unanticipated activities. For example, an employee might be performing a duty when cutting the grass at a faculty house even though that house is not on or abutting the campus. A person injured while playing softball on an informal faculty team on another school's campus on a Sunday afternoon might also have a compensable injury under worker's compensation, for it might be shown that faculty member's school encouraged such interscholastic faculty competitions.

FICA

The Federal Insurance Contribution Act requires a percentage of an employee's wages to be withheld and matched by the employer for what is more commonly known as "social security." The issue here is what constitutes wages. The independent school community has consistently claimed that providing school meals and school housing is done specifically for "the convenience of the employer" and thus does not constitute wages subject to FICA withholding.

This basic position was recently upheld by the U.S. Supreme Court in an analogous case not involving a school. If a school has been paying FICA on meals and lodging, it may file for a refund from the Internal Revenue Service. Because the IRS is contesting this issue in school settings, however, the school should place any refunds received in an escrow account until the matter is settled.

8.

The Development Office

Development officers need to be thoroughly familiar with the "product" they sell, with the competition for donors, with potential donors' interests, and with the legitimate tools available for fund raising. Development officers usually focus on the second and third items on this list, but some occasionally forget the first and last, where confusion and potential legal issues are most likely to arise.

As pointed out in Chapter 6, agents who represent the school must be knowledgeable because other people—in this case, donors—will rely on their representations, whether written or spoken. For instance, some donors may wish to back out if they suddenly discover that a school has changed substantially since "the good old days" or that a school's commitment to their particular interests is in fact minimal, even though an aggressive fund raiser has represented it as being substantial. Thus omissions in representations to donors may therefore be as important as negligent ones and lead to legal problems.

Just as admission officers can help curriculum committees by informing them about the pool of student talent, so may development officers help a board of trustees and administrators by passing on the inevitable criticisms that are made when the school tries to raise funds. A development officer's knowledge of precisely what the school stands for and offers is essential.

Publications

Advertising a school is a more delicate proposition than advertising most other products because of the emotional connection between the institution and its "extended family." The information in fund-raising speeches and brochures must therefore be accurate and complete for its particular purpose. It must be clear, for example, not only that the school plans to build a new gymnasium, but also that the school is going to maintain its emphasis on interscholastic, competitive athletics rather than reducing this emphasis and including more students in intramural sports. Why? Because the school is planning to build a gymnasium, a donor may really be paying for the opportunity of seeing the school defeat college freshman teams.

Donors are not the only people who will see these development materials and rely on them. Graduates who are recruiting, and potential applicants who are being recruited, will add the representations in a development brochure to their thinking about how the school recruits and about attending the school.

The Federal Trade Commission may regard such slogans as "the biggest little cement mixer in the world" as simple boasting. A school's representation that it "builds character" may arguably be only a boast, but a representation that it has "the best math and computer center in the country" had better be provable. If a brochure advertises something other than what the school presents, some donors may ask for their money back. Actually, every representation a school makes helps to form the basis of the bargain between a school and another party. Publications must therefore be consciously and carefully coordinated.

In addition to representing the school's program accurately, a development officer must also clearly understand the tools at hand to help a potential donor "build" a gift. Deferred giving, living wills, pooled income trusts, and the like are giving methods that are appropriate to some people but not others. Just as a will naming the school as beneficiary could be attacked if a development officer had witnessed it, a sophisticated giving method could be attacked if a donor's executor could show that the donor had been moved into entering into such an agreement by an enthusiastic development officer without appropriate advice in estate planning from his or her attorney or accountant. It is illegal for nonlawyers to practice law. Development officers must therefore be careful to tell donors to seek a lawyer's advice about legal issues.

Recipients

The "reliance theory" in pledging and giving gifts goes both ways. The donor relies on the school's representations, and the school relies on the contractual responsibility of the donor to make good on a pledge. Also, in certain circumstances, other donors might be able to demonstrate that they had relied on the sincerity of a "lead donor" when making their own pledges and that, because the lead donor's pledge had failed, so should theirs. Because of the negative political and public relations aspects of vigorous enforcement of pledges, lawsuits in this area are relatively rare — but they have succeeded, especially where the recipient institution can show that it has made commitments to third parties on the basis of donor X's pledge and where the presence of other donors was arguably attributable to donor X's willingness to contribute.

If the stock market falls, the family corporation fails, or a grandchild is expelled, donors who were previously happy may struggle to find ways to avoid meeting their pledges. Careful planning and communication by a development officer can, at the very least, make the decision whether to enforce a pledge a political rather than a legal consideration. For this reason, at least, development officers must keep accurate files of all materials and communications surrounding each gift.

Some possible pitfalls

A school must never be the knowing conduit for self-dealing or conflict of interest (discussed in Chapter 1 as these pertain to trustees). A school's desire for money may lead to a situation analogous to conflict of interest where, for example, it uses its charitable status to help "payers" become "donors" or "lenders" become "givers." An example of a payer becoming a donor is the noncustodial parent of a child receiving financial aid who is asked to and does pay the school what is actually tuition but is acknowledged by the school as a gift. An example of a lender becoming a giver is the trustee who "donates" stock in his or her closely held corporation but requires the school to retain the stock in its portfolio and thus retains control over the voting of the stock by being on the board of the school.

Donors must be competent to give, must have the present intent to give, the recipient must be willing to receive, and the donor must relinquish all dominion and control over the corpus of the gift for legally cognizable giving to be accomplished.

Another dangerous situation is created by publicizing the notion that "our school's tuitions are low because all parents donate generously to the school." This statement could be challenged by the Internal Revenue Service, which might try to compute what the actual per pupil costs are and then try not only to disallow parents' "gifts" but also to relieve the school of its tax-exempt status.

Volunteers

Schools, often through their development offices, generate volunteer programs, using parents' and graduates' energies to defray costs or to raise money for the institution. Here as elsewere the people recruited must be carefully screened, trained, and supervised. For example, what is said by a volunteer during a phonathon is presumed to be an authorized statement about the school and one on which a donor can reasonably rely.

Volunteers in a school's math lab or library must realize that they are agents of the school and that they and the school are liable for what they do. It makes good legal and business sense either to have volunteers who are well trained or no volunteers at all. From the business point of view, not only do trained volunteers do a better job; they also feel rewarded if they learn something in return for their labors. They feel truly part of the school and proud that it has cared enough to give them special training. This training should include, but not be limited to, orientation for the specific task, information about the school's discipline policies, information about personal tax deductibility (of travel expenses but not time, for example), and the potential of a defamation suit against the volunteer and the school if the volunteer abuses "inside information" about such things as families' finances or individual children.

9.

Town and Gown

Schools are communities unto themselves to a great extent, but not completely. Schools exist not only out of their traditions and in their hopes for their students' future worth to society but also in the present, real world.

A significant portion of that world is the municipality in which a school is located and with whose politicians, merchants, and police a school must deal. A school's ability to get rezoned a newly acquired parcel is, for example, a matter of law *and* politics. Legally, the parcel must be used for a permissible purpose — and, in this case, a nontaxable purpose — and the use must bear a substantial relation both to the law and to the town's health and welfare codes. These codes can be and are interpreted by townspeople.

How favorable that interpretation is depends in part on how each member of the "school family" has acted in the past. Just as trying to keep an errant student out of jail and under the school's disciplinary rules depends in part on good past relations with the police, other good-neighbor relations will have a great effect on the school's ability to succeed in gaining the confidence and cooperation of the town. Good-faith dealings and clear communication are vital to healthy town-gown relations.

Local police

Chapter 4 briefly describes how a school's involvement with local police can trigger standards of care that differ from those the school would otherwise apply on its own. This is not always true, of course, and cooperation with local police and probation officers can be fostered by such means as asking them to give drug information sessions or sessions on the law in general and by looking to them as *partners* with the school in knowing about the town's juvenile population and current concerns. In short, the school's relations with municipal authorities should be as cooperative as possible.

It is safe to say that a town's police force is more than happy to have a school retain jurisdiction over its students. The police will cooperate with this in mind as long as they know that appropriate restitution will be worked out between the school and, say, a store owner who has been the victim of shoplifting by students. Failing appropriate and successful responses by the school, however, the police will become increasingly likely to deal with even minor matters involving a school's students.

Town police have as much authority over students in a boarding school in that town as they do over any other persons who enjoy the benefits and protections of that town's laws.

Students' off-campus deportment

The extent to which a school is responsible for the deportment of its students off campus depends on the facts of each case. For example, a student who steals in a local store generally bears the responsibility for that action; the school does not. On the other hand, the civil or criminal acts of students off campus but during a school-supervised activity may well lead to complaints against the school for negligent supervision. Yet other examples include damages that result from an overaggressive athlete or a student possessing acid taken from the school's laboratory. In both instances, the school may be liable for its negligence in encouraging or allowing such dangerous situations to develop.

Many day and boarding schools have been moved to issue detailed statements on their positions on the off-campus deportment of students in circumstances where students are sports spectators, attending dances, at local bars, and even at parties at their own houses. A school must carefully consider how willing and able it is to enforce such guidelines in a way that is consistent with its published rules, regulations, and procedures. It must also consider that it may be held liable for students' off-campus behavior to the degree that it advertises that it holds itself responsible for such behavior.

Epilogue

Most independent school people feel a keen responsibility for the intellectual and personal development of their students in and out of school. They also recognize that the presence of students is the only justification for their schools.

It is sad when families feel they must resort to litigation to resolve differences between their children and their children's schools when the parties, given their ages and experiences, have entered into relationships based on the loftiest of motives and values.

The purpose of this "primer" is to help people in schools strike a realistic balance between lofty objectives and the methods of meeting those objectives in the real world. We hope that this book will help readers to anticipate and thus avoid potential legal consequences that can and do arise when the pressure of practical problems encroaches on sincerely held beliefs about how young people ought to learn and grow.

Appendix A

Glossary of Legal Terms

accident. An event that occurs without fault, carelessness, or want of circumspection concerning the person affected; not a technical legal term.

arbitrary. Without reason given; not supported by fair, solid, and substantial cause.

assault. Threat of harm, putting victim in immediate apprehension for safety.

battery. Unlawful or unconsented-to touching or other wrongful physical violence or constraint without another's consent.

breach of duty. Failure to fulfill the duty owed to another.

burden of proof. The onus that must be borne by a party in litigation in order to go forward with all or part of a case.

capricious. Sudden and unpredictable; without just cause.

charter. An act of the legislature or articles of incorporation creating a corporation and defining its purposes, privileges, powers, rights, and franchise.

civil action. An action instituted to compel payment or to do some other thing that is purely civil (that is, not criminal) in nature; an action to establish or recover or for redress of private and civil rights.

civil rights. Rights appertaining to a person by virtue of his or her citizenship in a state or community; rights capable of being enforced or redressed in a civil action (see above); certain rights secured to all citizens of the United States by the Fifth and Fourteenth amendments to the Constitution and by various acts of Congress made in pursuance thereof.

common law. The body of legal principles that derives authority from the judgment of the state and federal courts.

contract. A promissory agreement between two or more persons that creates, modifies, or destroys a legal relation; an agreement, upon sufficient consideration, to do or not to do a certain thing; may be written, oral, or implied (see "quasi contract," below).

contributory negligence. Negligence of the plaintiff, which, coupled with that of the defendant, constitutes proximate cause (see below) of the injury complained of.

corporation. An artificial person or legal entity, created by or under the authority of laws of a state or nation, with personality and existence distinct from its members and with continuous succession.

defamation. Words spoken or written that have the effect, on publication, of injuring a person's reputation; includes libel and slander (see below).

defendant. The person defending or denying the accusation of offense; the person against whom recovery or relief is sought in an action or suit brought by a plaintiff (or by a prosecutor in a criminal action).

doctrine. Used in this text to mean a common law principal or theory generally accepted by courts.

due diligence and care. The accepted standard of attention and good judgment required to protect other persons or their property under specific conditions.

due process. Procedural fairness.

endowment. A gift of a permanent fund to a school, hospital, university, charity, etc.

equal protection. Similar treatment of people similarly situated.

equity. Equal or impartial justice between persons whose rights or claims are in conflict; justice as ascertained by reason and ethical insight but independent of the formulated body of law; fairness.

fiduciary. One who is responsible to another person or institution that has a right to rely on one's good faith, skill, and good judgment; a fiduciary owes a high degree of diligence and care to the person or property entrusted to it.

good faith. An honest attempt to deal honestly with another.

harm. Injury to persons physically or emotionally, or to property.

indemnification. Generally, the result of an agreement by one party (often an insurance company) to pay costs incurred by another party and o wed to a third party under certain agreed-upon circumstances.

injury. See "harm," above.

in loco parentis. Standing in place of the parent.

liability. Exposure for failure to fulfill an obligation to another that one is bound in law or justice to perform.

libel. Written words of a nature that, upon publication, injure the reputation of another by bringing him or her into disdain or contempt or ridicule.

litigation. Judicial controversy.

malfeasance. Performance of an act that is wholly wrongful and unlawful.

misfeasance. Performance of an act that might lawfully be done, but in an improper manner, by which another person receives an injury.

negligence. Failure to do what a person of ordinary prudence and foresight might be expected to do and that through a duty owed forms the proximate cause (see below) of an injury to another.

nonfeasance. Nonperformance of an act that ought to be performed.

plaintiff. The party bringing the action in a court of law.

police power. The power of the state to control the health, welfare, comfort, and prosperity of its people.

proximate cause. That which in its natural consequence, unbroken by any intervening cause, produces an injury and without which the injury would not have occurred.

quasi contract. As if a contract had been effected.

reasonable. Just, proper, customary under the circumstances.

respondeat superior. Tort doctrine standing for a superior's accountability for the unlawful or otherwise negligent acts of his or her agent in the course of the agent's scope of employment.

slander. Malicious defamation of a person's reputation, profession, or business by spoken words.

standard of care. Statutes, common law, and/or custom and usage in the performance of a particular duty that prescribe the quality of performance of the duty owed and become "the standard."

state action. A term invoked when an otherwise private enterprise becomes so entangled with the state through the state's contribution or control that the activity loses its private identity (a court finding of state action brings constitutional standards to bear on the relationship between the enterprise and individuals).

statute. Law enacted by the legislative power in a country or state.

theory. See "doctrine," above.

tort. An actionable wrong or injury to another; a civil, or noncriminal, act or omission.

Appendix B

Index to NAIS Legislative Memoranda

Periodically since 1970 NAIS has issued legislative memoranda to member schools on a variety of topics. These memoranda detail the evolution of many of the issues reflected in this book. Although this index may date the book somewhat, we offer it in the belief that interested readers may wish to refer to specific memoranda or to ask the NAIS library for up-to-date information on specific topics. The index is arranged alphabetically by subject heading, with the titles of memoranda and dates of issue listed beneath.

Charitable deductions

Fisher-Conable Bill (H.R. 11183) To Expand Charitable Deductions   *3/29/78*

Disallowance of Charitable Contributions from Parents   *10/23/79*

Charitable Deductions for Nonitemizers   *4/10/80*

Deductibility of Parent Contributions   *4/10/80*

Charitable Contributions   *9/26/80*

Charitable Contributions Legislation (To Extend the Charitable Deduction to Nonitemizing Taxpayers)   *5/22/81*

Charitable Deduction for Nonitemizing Taxpayers Becomes Law   *8/13/81*

Deductibility of Parent Contributions   *3/83*

Collective bargaining

Letter to Board Chairmen from Chairman of Trustee Committee on Personnel Policies   *12/11/75*

Personnel Relations in an Era of Collective Bargaining   *12/11/75*

Copyright law

The Copyright Revision Act Relative to Musical Performances   *7/21/78*

Guidelines for Off-Air Recording of Broadcast Programming for Educational Purposes   *3/82*

Energy conservation grants

Energy Conservation Grants   *4/10/79*

ERISA (Employee Retirement Income Security Act of 1974)

Memorandum 1: Employee Retirement Income Security Act of 1974   *10/29/74*

Memorandum 2: NAIS Counsel's Memorandum Reviewing Requirements, etc.   *12/19/74*

Memorandum 3: Plan Termination Insurance, Fiduciary Responsibilities, Bonding, Reporting and Disclosure, Claims Procedure, and Tax-qualification Requirements   *5/7/75*

Memorandum 4: Extension of Postponement, Fiduciary Responsibility, and Changes in Filing Requirements for Form EBS-1   *7/16/75*

Memorandum 5: Deadline for Amending Plans   *12/3/75*

Memorandum 6: Plan Description Form EBS-1, Filing, and Deferral of Summary Plan Description Requirements   *5/21/76*

Federal food programs

Descriptions of the Various Food Programs   *12/70*

Update on Federal Food Programs   *9/75*

School Food Program and the Handicapped   *4/10/79*

Agriculture Department—Child Nutrition Programs   *3-4/81*

Elimination of Eligibility of Some Private Schools in Child Nutrition Programs   *8/13/81*

Safety standards for school buses
New Safety Standards for School Buses   *7/21/78*

Sex discrimination
Discrimination Laws and the Independent School (Title VII of the Civil Rights Act as Amended by the Equal Opportunity Act of 1972)   *10/21/74*
Title IX Regulations   *9/19/75*
Sex Equality in Employee Benefit Plans   *9/19/78*
Sex Equality in Employee Benefit Plans   *11/13/78*
Discrimination Due to Pregnancy   *4/10/79*
Discrimination Due to Pregnancy   *6/4/79*
Sex Discrimination in Pension Benefits   *12/31/80*
Sex Discrimination in Employment Banned   *5/82*

Student rights
Discipline and Due Process   *4/9/76*
Discipline and Due Process—Memorandum No. 2   *4/27/77*

"Sunset" legislation
"Sunset" Proposals   *5/15/80*
"Sunset" for Tax Expenditures, including Tax Exemption and the Charitable Deduction and Summary Statement of Testimony for S.219   *6/13/80*
"Sunset" Legislation   *8/26/80*
"Sunset" Clause in Charitable Deduction Bill   *8/13/81*

Tax reform
Tax Reform Bill   *8/25/69*
Tax Reform Bill—Update   *9/29/69*
Summary of Tax Reform Legislation   *8/8/70*
Tax Reform Proposals Affecting Charitable Contributions   *3/21/73*
Tax Reform 1975   *1/9/75*
Tax Reform and Charitable Contributions   *7/7/75*
Progress Report on Tax Reform Legislation   *10/8/75*
Tax Reform and the Summer of 1977   *6/28/77*
Expected Changes Due to Passage of Economic Recovery Tax Act   *8/13/81*

Tuition remission
Tax Treatment of Tuition Remission   *8/11/72*
Revision Expected by IRS on Tuition Remission Programs   *2/21/73*
Proposed IRS Revision on Tuition Remission   *11/16/76*
Tuition Remission: IRS Proposed Regulation   *1/19/77*
Taxation of Tuition Remission   *3-4/81*

Tuition tax relief
Legislation to Provide Tax Credits   *4/12/72*

About the Author

Albrecht Saalfield, a graduate of Phillips Exeter Academy (N.H.), has served as a teacher and administrator in independent schools and was head of Greenwich Country Day School (Conn.) from 1972 to 1975. He now practices law in Concord, Massachusetts.